Celebrating Pigs in the City

CINCINNATI · COVINGTON · NEWPORT

The Big Pig Gig

Celebrating Pigs in the City

ORANGE FRAZER PRESS

Wilmington, Ohio

ISBN 1-882203-70-4

Copyright ©2000 Art Opportunities, Incorporated

Published by Orange Frazer Press, Wilmington, Ohio

Text: Rick Pender
Foreword: Laura Pulfer
Photography:
Principal photographer: Javier E. Jarrin
Additional photographers: Tony Arrasmith
                              Robert A. Flischel
                              Thomas W. Guenther
                              Joe Harrison
                              Peggy McHale
                              Kelly Barhhorst-Schnelle
                              Chris Cone

Design, setting, logotype: Dale Lamson
Editor: Tamara Harkavy

1st edition

Library of Congress Cataloging-in-Publication Data

The big pig gig : celebrating pigs in the city, Cincinnati,
Covington, Newport / {Text,
Rick Pender ; principal photographer, Javier E. Jarrin}.
        p.cm.
    Published on the occasion of the Big Pig Gig event to show
        case more than 400
    Decorated fiberglass lifesized pigs created by ArtWorks.
        Includes index.
        ISBN 1-882203-70-4
        1.Swine in art-Ohio-Cincinnati Region. 2. Public
    sculpture-Ohio-Cincinnati
    Region I.Pender,Rick, 1949- II. Artworks (program)
    NB1042.S85 B54 2000
    730'.9771'78-dc21   00-063707

For more information on ordering this book contact:
Orange Frazer Press
37 1/2 W. Main St.
P.O. Box 214
Wlimington, Ohio 45177
1-800-852-9332
www.orangefrazer.com
www.bigpiggig.com

Printed in Canada

JAVIER E. JARRIN

JAVIER E. JARRIN

This book is dedicated to everyone who embraced the joy and spirit of The Big Pig Gig.

(Histay ookbay isay edicatedday otay everyoneay howay embraceday hetay oyjay anday piritsay ofay hetay igBay igPig igGay.)

Acknowledgements

There is no question about it.

The Big Pig Gig was a tremendous success. Visitors came to Greater Cincinnati, and people came downtown to see the pigs. It helped bridge the Ohio River. It raised money for deserving charities. And, most importantly, it was fun!

And to think it all started here when Laura Pulfer wrote a column about Alexander Longi, an 8 year-old with a "pig" idea.

The obvious people to thank are the artists and sponsors, without whom the Big Pig Gig could not have happened. However, hundreds more organizations and individuals contributed time, talent and resources to make the Big Pig Gig the tremendous community event that it was.

The Big Pig Gig received unparalleled community support, starting with sponsors, who agreed that this would be fun and good for our community, and so signed on to buy pigs. They didn't just buy pigs, though. They talked about their pigs, they named their pigs, they had parties around their pigs, and they made their pig part of their summer.

Starting with a clean, newborn fiberglass pig created by our fabricators, Glass Hand and Glasgo, artists put their creative minds to work and submitted more than 1,000 possible pig designs. The selected artists spent countless hours preparing their pigs, and then repairing them if necessary.

Beyond thanking the sponsors and artists, though, it is important that several individuals and groups be thanked by name for their role in this tremendous community event. At the top is the Big Pig Gig Steering Committee. Before anyone else had heard of the Big Pig Gig or knew what a success the Big Pig Gig would be, the Steering Committee, including Joan Kaup, Mark Serianne, Karen Maier, Sue Ernst, Eric Avner, Randy

Smith, Cheryl Curtis, Rick Greiwe, David Ginsburg, Jim Tarbell, Kelly Weissmann, Charles Desmarais, Ron Felder, Dave Dougherty and Joyce Monger, worked tirelessly to ensure an inclusive, fun and successful event.

The Gig would not have happened without the approval and cooperation of the local governments. Thanks go to the City of Cincinnati, the office of Mayor Charlie Luken, the Cincinnati Park Board, the Cincinnati Recreation Commission, and the Departments of Safety, Architecture, and Facility Management, and to Carol Walker who helped the Gig staff navigate through these many city departments. Thanks also to the City of Newport, and the City of Covington and downtown building owners and managers hosting pigs.

Lamson Design, Joan Kaup, and Northlich lead the charge early on, getting the word out, designing and producing pig sales brochures and the call for artists. Hundreds of volunteers were recruited and scheduled by Rosemary Cwiok. Cindy Biddinger and Julie Maslov chaired a Public Relations Committee of more than a dozen people. The Marketing Committee involved another group of dedicated volunteers. Sara Vance and Jackie Reau led the effort to involve area media. Anastasia Mileham and Nancy Parrott facilitated the involvement of downtown businesses in the Big Pig Gig. Eric Avner, Cheryl Curtis, Sue Ernst and Marcia Shortt managed the Hogistics of pig placement. Tracy Tucker organized and led the Boar Guide tour program. Janel Carrol ensured that the bills were paid on time. Janet Hill Smith developed special events.

Lamson Design created the logo and design of Big Pig Gig materials. The Big Pig Gig maps were produced and distributed with help from xpedx, Frisch's, and SpringDot. The Greater Cincinnati Convention and Visitors Bureau was a key partner in the regional, national and international marketing of the Big Pig Gig. Arizona Ice Tea donated a clipping service to track the tremendous volume of print media that the Big Pig Gig received. Frisch's Restaurants was a key distribution point for our Tour de Pork maps.

The Big Pig Gig website was designed and maintained pro-bono by MPI Studio. Owners Joshua Barnes and David Jepson spent countless hours working with Gig volunteers Deborah Haupert and Mitch Dunn to create an informative and entertaining site that was one of the main marketing tools of the Big Pig Gig. Ginny Segbers also deserves our thanks for her role in getting www.BigPigGig.com started.

In the true spirit of community, many local media outlets put aside competitive differences and supported the Big Pig Gig. Time Warner Cable, WKRC Channel 12, WLWT Channel 5, WCET Channel 48 and Media Bridges gave air time, and WLWT Channel 5 and 12 Creative Services gave TV production services. Radio stations B105, WGUC, MoJo, and WLW all partnered with the Big Pig Gig. *The Cincinnati Enquirer*, (especially Owen Findsen and his daily pig profiles) *Cincinnati Post, CityBeat,* the *Downtowner, 50 Plus, Cincinnati Magazine* and *All About Kids* and *Cincinnati Woman's Magazine* all supported the Big Pig Gig with promotional efforts.

The pigs would not be on the streets without major help from City Dash and other local businesses. Completed pigs were dropped off at City Dash, and City Dash vehicles were used by Pig Planting teams. Concrete Technologies, Inc. donated the more than 400 bases. Cinergy Corp. loaned trucks, Convergys donated computers for the office staff, and hog-calling was made possible by Cincinnati Bell Wireless. Jack Rouse and Associates, Towne Properties and Central Parking Systems donated space to the Big Pig Gig.

Big Pig Gig merchandise was developed and sold with the help of many "Gig Gear" partners. Lamson Design, Westerman Printing, Lori Siebert, Josh and Katie Baker all contributed product design to the Gig gear mix.

Several area foundations gave funds to broaden the base of organizations that could be involved. The Greater Cincinnati Foundation offered matching grants for small businesses and non-profits. KnowledgeWorks Foundation, bigg's, Benefactors and the Louise Taft Semple Foundation made the participation of more than 50 schools possible.

The unsung heroes of the Big Pig Gig, the staff, who patiently sorted through the details of producing this major community event, should be thanked. This group of energetic people gave their time and energy to the community and truly made this event a success. Megan Jefferson, Betsy Neyer, Mike Uhlenhake, Kim Humphries, Joyce Monger, Julie Mayer, Amanda Hogan, Sara Arndt, Sarah Lathi, Javier Jarrin, Cathy Wash and Jennifer Schneider, as well as the Pig Planting Teams lead by P. J. Grady, Bob Kennicott and John Hand pulled it all together and make the Big Pig Gig a success.

There are dozens to whom we're indebted for their help, support, and enthusiasm, whose names do not appear in print. To all of you, we say, "a pig thank you."

Melody Sawyer Richardson
Co-Chair

Tamara Harkavy
Executive Director

Joe Hale
Co-Chair

Table of Contents

Foreword

It began with Chicago's cows.

A life-sized, colorfully painted fiberglass herd roamed the streets of the Windy City, the coolest thing about the blistering summer of 1999. A tarted-up Carmen Mooranda in fishnet stockings. Burly cows in hard hats. Cows on wheels. Cows on skates.

Cincinnati tourists suffered briefly from a case of bovine envy. But, a proud and resourceful people, we quickly decided that pigs are a completely superior canvas. Not to mention the funniest animal in the barnyard. For every bad cow pun, there are a hundred bad puns about pigs.

We were udderly determined to hog the limelight. Was it art? Or commerce? The people who get things done in town chose to believe that it might be both. Arts patron Melody Sawyer Richardson, Cinergy Foundation President Joe Hale and ArtWorks Director Tamara Harkavy took the pig by the snout — raising the first $50,000 in seed money and tapping artists, educators, business executives and public servants to work with them. More than fifty schools with hundreds of teachers and aspiring artists joined. The Big Pig Gig was up and snorting.

Hundreds of artists were engaged, including aspiring artists from fifty-three schools. About 400 pigs eventually made their way from Covington to Newport to Cincinnati's Fountain Square and Union Terminal and Eden Park. Some flew. Some reared up on their hind legs. Some lit up. Some were beautiful — stunning really. Some were painted in the style of an already-known artist: Pigasso, Pigtisse,

Roy Lichtenswine. Others were totally original. Some were funny. Some carried a message.

A lot was riding on these little cloven hooves, and, as promised, the porkers brought home the bacon. Besides showcasing regional talent, The Gig resulted in an estimated $170 million boost to the local economy. More than 500,000 visitors came to town, leaving behind money at hotels, restaurants and stores.

This is not to calculate the intangibles. People from the suburbs, the exurbs and neighboring towns — who hadn't had a reason to come downtown for years — came to see the pigs. With cameras. With kids. Downtown workers took the long way to the parking lot at the end of the day — looking for new pigs.

And the summer of 2000 became the summer of the pig. A reason to come downtown. A reason to cheerfully ignore the construction mess. A reason to smile.

— Laura Pulfer

JAVIER E. JARRIN

The Big Pig Gig

Celebrating Pigs in the City

CINCINNATI • COVINGTON • NEWPORT

Why Pigs?

Cincinnati's Proud Porkopolis Past

People smile about the idea of a "Big Pig Gig." But Cincinnati would not be the city it is without pigs.

Early in the 19th century farmers in the country surrounding the city raised pigs and corn, a combination that produced excellent meat and livelihood for the many German people emigrating to the city.

By the 1820s, the bustling port of Cincinnati made it possible to transport pork more rapidly to consumer markets. Cincinnati businesses sprang up around the pork-packing industry.

It was not uncommon for pigs to be herded through the streets in the 1830s and 1840s. They were smelly and made a mess of the streets. Visitors were often shocked, but Cincinnatians grew used to them, erecting sturdy wrought-iron fences to keep the pigs off their city properties.

So much of the meat came from Cincinnati that the city began to be jokingly called "Porkopolis." In 1835 the city was the leading meat-packing center in America. By 1845 it led the world.

The pork-packing industry led to other new businesses. Hog bristles were used in plaster and to make brushes, mattresses and furniture. Tanneries used hides to make boots, shoes and saddles. Pork fat was used to make lamps oil and candles.

A candle-maker, James Gamble, partnered with businessman William Procter in 1837 to use pork fat to produce a high-quality soap and sell it in small blocks. From those humble beginnings grew the Procter & Gamble Company, one of the largest consumer product manufacturers in the world today.

In 1988 when Cincinnati celebrated its bicentennial with the installation of a family park on the river, Sawyer Point, sculptor Andrew Leicester conceived a whimsical set of statues to mark the city's roots at the park's entrance. High atop four smokestacks, fashioned like those on the steamboats that once plied the Ohio River, are four pigs with wings.

The expression, "when pigs fly" usually means an impossible task. But in Cincinnati, where local citizens have a soft spot for the animals who changed the course of local history, it's a sign that exciting things are happening.

The Big Pig Gig was a community-wide public art event celebrating Cincinnati's Porkopolis heritage by showcasing emerging and established local artists, supporting tourism and promoting regional partnerships. Ultimately more than 400 decorated fiberglass pigs hogged the streets of Greater Cincinnati and Northern Kentucky during the summer of 2000. The Big Pig Gig was a production of ARTWORKS, an award-winning arts-based employment and job training program for youth in the Greater Cincinnati region.

JAVIER E. JARRIN

Calling all hogs

The sponsorship/artist kick-off and other porcine delights

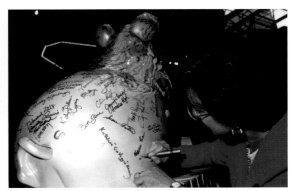

Working like a dog on pigs.

Artists go whole hog on incredible concepts.

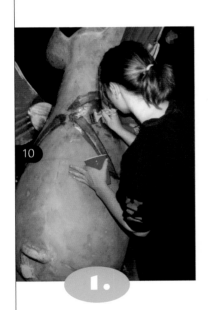

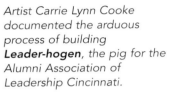

*Artist Carrie Lynn Cooke documented the arduous process of building **Leader-hogen**, the pig for the Alumni Association of Leadership Cincinnati.*

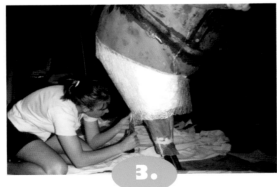

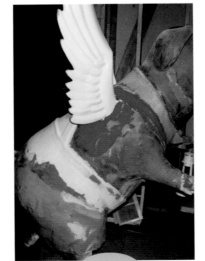

7.

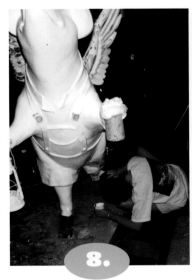

8.

9.

10.

11.

Yes!

Now get that hog in its pen.

Installation can be like wrestling a greased pig.

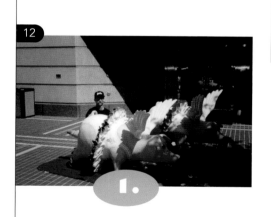

*The pig planting team works with artist T A Boyle to install **Swine Lake**.*

World's Largest Pignic

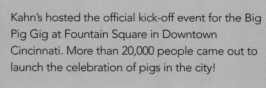

Kahn's hosted the official kick-off event for the Big Pig Gig at Fountain Square in Downtown Cincinnati. More than 20,000 people came out to launch the celebration of pigs in the city!

June 10, 2000

15

ArtWorks creates the Big Little Pig Gig

Imagine a place teeming with creativity, youthful enthusiasm, and intense concentration. ArtWorks is just such a place. It is Cincinnati's summer job training and employment program for talented teenagers, that imparts meaningful work-skills through the arts. Located under the big white tents at Eden Park for eight weeks during the summer, ArtWorks participants earn a paycheck while learning to be productive, creative members of tomorrow's workforce. In the process they create works of art for sale or public display that expresses who they are—leaving no doubt about all they are capable of becoming.

The Big Little Pig Gig was one of eight ArtWorks 2000 projects. Apprentices worked all summer to create little pigs, their contribution to the Big Pig Gig. These colorful and creative piglets were sold at the annual ArtWorks fundraiser.

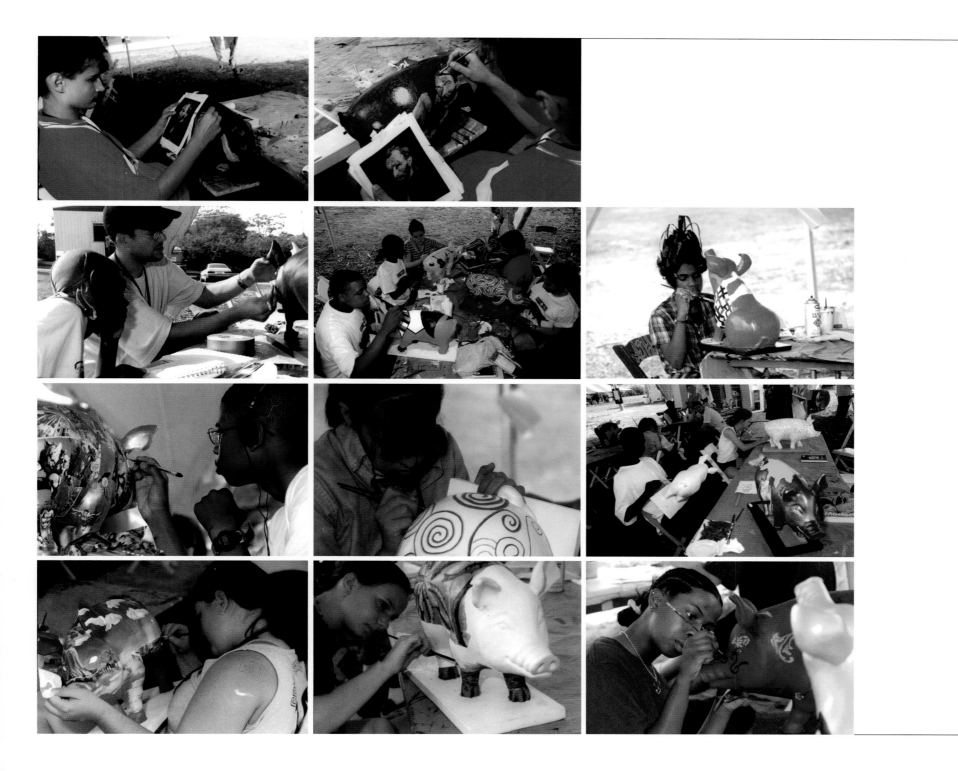

The Sowlon

PAINTED PIGS BECAME A NEW ART FORM, ESPECIALLY THOSE CELEBRATING

PAINTERS, SCULPTORS AND DESIGNERS FROM AROUND THE WORLD AND

ACROSS THE CENTURIES.

19

Previous page:

PIGLETXANDER CALDER
Joel Selmeier
Trustees of the Cincinnati Art
Museum

Left to right:

DAVID HOGNEY
Students of Althea Thompson
Photography by Jacqui Phlipot
John Morrell & Co.
for School for Creative and
Performing Arts

PIGALL
Ellen Miller
Patricia A. Vance Foundation &
Karen F. Maier

JAVIER E. JARRIN

JAVIER E. JARRIN

PEGGY McHALE

JAVIER E. JARRIN

Clockwise, from the top left:

VINCENT VAN HOGH
Walter L. Gross III
Walter L. Gross, Jr. & Family

PIGTISSE
Holly Schapker
SMV Media (Sara M. Vance)

ROY LICHTENSWINE (SORRY, ROY)
Kevin Kelly
Volunteers of the Cincinnati Art Museum

PIGASSO
Judy Anderson
Lynn and Tom Cooney

JAVIER E. JARRIN

JAVIER E. JARRIN

22

JAVIER E. JARRIN

At left:

PORCINE PORC-ELAIN
Ted Gantz (sculptor) and Marlene Steele (painter)
Genevieve Hilmer for the Taft Museum of Art

JAVIER E. JARRIN

JAVIER E. JARRIN

Clockwise, from top left:

HAMRI MATISSE

Mary Beth Dowlin
Amgen
The Barrett Cancer Center,
University of Cincinnati

CAM HAM

Patrick Sr., Patrick Jr., and Thomas Romelli
Romelli Design, Inc.

JOINK MIRO

Northwest Art Club
Fluor Daniel Fernald/Baker
Concrete/Huber General
Contracting/Berchie
Holliday/Northwest HS Art
Club,Students and Faculty
Northwest High School

JAVIER E. JARRIN

Left to right:

SOWN MIRO
Students of Louise Hausman: Shannon Lawrence, Noah Allen, Audrey DeYoung, Alison Hontanosas, Dan Long, Austin Mitchell/Students of Julia Emark: Louie Horn, Jenni Legere, Josh Johns
Louise Taft Semple Foundation for Cincinnati Country Day School (Upper School) and St. Bernard/Elmwood Place High School

PIG DREAMS I
Bryan Joiner
ACME Construction Services

Far right:

POP PIG - ANDY WARHOG
T.A. Boyle
Volunteers of the Cincinnati Art Museum

JAVIER E. JARRIN

JAVIER E. JARRIN

25

Clockwise, from top left:

GOLDIE HOCKS - HOW GREAT SOW ART
John A. Ruthven
Shannon and Lee Carter for the
Fine Arts Fund

MICHAELHAMGELO
8th Grade Artists of Sycamore Junior High School
Sycamore Junior High School

SALVADOR PIGALI
Tess Little
Hans French and Michele Fries
d/b/a French Fries

PIGGIN' OUT ON ART!
Helen Needles
50 Plus Magazine

JAVIER E. JARRIN

JAVIER E. JARRIN

KELLY SCHNELLE

JAVIER E. JARRIN

JAVIER E. JARRIN

At left:

HIS DREAMS TOOK HIM ON A
COLORFUL JOURNEY
Leslee Wick
The Wilson Art Stores, inc.

KELLY BARNHORST-SCHNELLE

Top to bottom:

PIGGY MAX

Deirdre Mahne
Bristol-Myers Squibb Oncology and
SmithKline Beecham Oncology
for the The Barrett Cancer Center,
University of Cincinnati

GREAT AMERICAN SWINE ART

Mark Eberhard
August A. Rendigs Foundation, W.
Roger Fry, Trustee
Great American Artists

Opposite page:

SWINE ART

Art Stop Kids
Ashland, Inc. Foundation for
The Carnegie Visual and Performing
Arts Center

JOE HARRISON

KELLY BARNHORST-SCHNELLE

Hog Futures

IN HARDWORKING CINCINNATI, EVERYONE PULLED TOGETHER TO MAKE

PRODUCTIVE PIGS. TECHNO PIGS. DOT-COM PIGS. CORPORATE PIGS. THEY

WERE PULLING THEIR WEIGHT.

31

JAVIER E. JARRIN

JAVIER E. JARRIN

Previous page:

2 SOWSEND

Joshua Thomas
The Art Institute of Cincinnati
(formerly ACA College of Design)

Clockwise, from top Left:

PORKFOLIO BY PNC

Bill Lawley
PNC for the
The Carnegie Arts Center

SOWND INVESTOR

Merle Rosen
Ohio National Financial Services

THE FIFTH THIRD PIGGY BANK

Lamson Design
Fifth Third Bank

JAVIER E. JARRIN

JAVIER E. JARRIN

JAVIER E. JARRIN

JAVIER E. JARRIN

Clockwise, from top left:

TYPIGRAPHIC
Sanger & Eby Design
Sanger & Eby Design

BRINGIN' HOME THE BACON
Bradford McDougall
Lyons & Fries Co., L.P.A.

SOW JONES
Kim Popil
Donahue Companies

33

JAVIER E. JARRIN

Clockwise, from top left:

CPA (CERTIFIED PIGLET ACCOUNTANT)
Lorraine Crooks
Grant Thornton LLP

CYBOARG
Jason Tingler
IAMS

PIGGEY.COM
Beth Hilton, Lawrence Hilton, Stephanie Unterhaslberg, Max Unterhaslberg
Ernst & Young

MEDIA HOG
Steve Brauch & Steve McGowan
Clear Channel Television & Radio for the Neediest Kids of All

JAVIER E. JARRIN

JAVIER E. JARRIN

JAVIER E. JARRIN

JAVIER E. JARRIN

ROBERT A. FLISCHEL

At left:

E-PIGGY.COM
Anthony Becker
Taft, Stettinius & Hollister LLP
Main Street Ventures

35

Left to right:

TYPIGRAPHY
Richards Group Artists
Richards Group Inc.

HAM SALAD
Mary Ann Reed
The Kroger Co.

JAVIER E. JARRIN

JAVIER E. JARRIN

JAVIER E. JARRIN

Clockwise, from top left:

ADBUSTER PIG
Douglas P. Smith
Lightborne, Inc.

THE CEO
Corey Jefferson
coolsavings.com

THE MESSENGER
Sam Hollingsworth
Priority Dispatch

JAVIER E. JARRIN

JOE HARRISON

At left:

ALAN GREENSPAM
Students of Donna Luggen
A.G. Edwards & Sons for
Clark Montessori

38

JAVIER E. JARRIN

JAVIER E. JARRIN

Clockwise, from top left:

HOG TIDE
Vernon Rader
Tide

CHAMBOAR OF COMMERCE
Thomas S. Owen
Greater Cincinnati Chamber of
Commerce

LINK
Greg Storer
Cincinnati Bell
Cincinnati Bell Wireless

DEADLINE SWINE
The Glass Hand
City Dash

JAVIER E. JARRIN

JAVIER E. JARRIN

Clockwise, from top left:

CERTIFIED PORK ACCOUNTANT
Eric Reed Greiner
KPMG LLP

HOGGING THE MARKET
Claude Spires
Fidelity Investments

HIGH ON THE HOG
Barbara Kelsch
Bartlett & Co.

Opposite:

BOARRISTER
David C. Smith
Dinsmore & Shohl LLP

JAVIER E. JARRIN

ROBERT A. FLISCHEL

JAVIER E. JARRIN

JAVIER E. JARRIN

Who you callin' "PIG"?

SOMETIMES IT WASN'T ENOUGH TO BE A PIG. BUT THAT WAS OK, BECAUSE IN A YEAR OF BIG

IMAGINATION, A PIG COULD BE ALMOST ANYTHING. HOW'S THAT FOR PIG POTENTIAL?

At left:

ERECTHEHAM ON THE PORKCROPOLIS
Donald Beck
Beck Architecture/Donald Beck/Lawrence Eynon M.D.

JAVIER E. JARRIN

JAVIER E. JARRIN

Left to right:

THE BUTTON GLUTTON
Students of Kat Rakel-Ferguson lead by Marissa Lin
Sycamore High School, Sycamore Community Schools

MERSOWDES
Jason Tingler
Mercedes-Benz of Cincinnati

PIG IN A POKE
Vernon Rader
Duro Bag Mfg. Co.

COVINGTON RETRIEVER
Wolfgang A. Ritschel
The Friends of Covington/Cincinnati Bell

KELLY BARNHORST- SCHNELLE

KELLY BARNHORST- SCHNELLE

JAVIER E. JARRIN

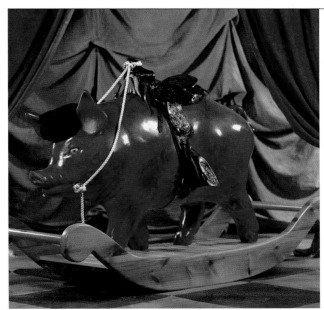

TONY ARRASMITH

45

JAVIER E. JARRIN

JAVIER E. JARRIN

Clockwise, from top left:

COW-ABUNGA
Julie Riehle (designed by Bryan Kopp)
Provident Bank

NEWPIG AQUARIUM
*Glen Este Middle School Students of
Lewis Cisle and Julie Chambers*
bigg's Eastgate for
Glen Este Middle School

HAM SWEET HAM
Sarah Lahti
Sibcy Cline Realtors

PORKUPINE
Zoe Hutton and Catherine Duffy
Sena, Weller, Rohs, Williams, Inc.

46

JAVIER E. JARRIN

JAVIER E. JARRIN

JAVIER E. JARRIN

JAVIER E. JARRIN

JAVIER E. JARRIN

JAVIER E. JARRIN

Clockwise, from top left:

CHOP 'TIL YOU DROP
Sanger & Eby Design
Federated Department Stores, Inc.

HOG WIRED
Richards Group Artists
BICCGeneral

METAMORPHOSWINE
John Maggard
Mercy Health Partners

O SOWLO MEEEEEO
Stephen Geddes
Convergys

47

JAVIER E. JARRIN

JAVIER E. JARRIN

At left:

KAHN-VERSATION PIECE
Bill Seitz
Hillshire Farm & Kahn's

JAVIER E. JARRIN

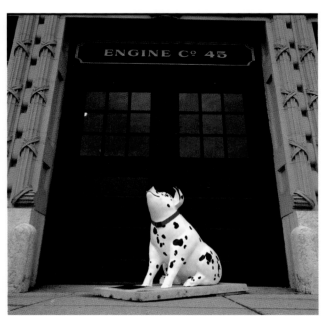

JAVIER E. JARRIN

JAVIER E. JARRIN

Clockwise, from top left:

ROAD HOG
Jim "Dauber" Farr
The Wood Family

PIGASAURUS
Patricia A. Renick
KnowledegeWorks

WHEN PIGS FLY
David A. Oehler
Cincinnati Zoo & Botanical Gardens

SPORKY
Thomas S. Owen
Cincinnati Fire Museum

49

JAVIER E. JARRIN

THOMAS W. GUENTHER

At left:

TOYOTA HAMRY
Jim "Dauber" Farr
Toyota Motor Manufacturing North
America, Inc.

Opposite:

GLOBAL PIG
Michael Sharp
Globe Furniture Galleries

50

"TOYOTA HAMRY"

BY: JIM "DAUBER" FARR

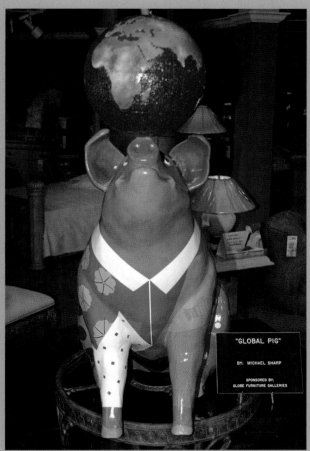

THOMAS W. GUENTHER

SPORKS

FROM HOOPS AND HARDBALLS TO, YOU GUESSED IT, PIGSKINS! OUR PIGS WERE GOOD SPORKS.

JAVIER E. JARRIN

Clockwise, from top left:

PIG RED MACHINE
Lynn Judd
Henry W. and Anita R. Schneider

MARATHON PIG
Mark Brawley
The Lottery Channel
The Flying Pig Marathon

PIG ON A RAMPAGE
Angela Smith, Katie Baker, Justin McCollum and Matt Hildebrand
Our Adopt-A-School Partners:
Matandy Steel, Cisle Inc./Tomson Steel for
Stephen T. Badin High School

PIGSKIN
John Wilson
Cincinnati Bengals

53

JAVIER E. JARRIN

JAVIER E. JARRIN

JAVIER E. JARRIN

54

JAVIER E. JARRIN

JAVIER E. JARRIN

JAVIER E. JARRIN

JAVIER E. JARRIN

Opposite:

A SLIDE OF HAM
Bev Kirk (concept by Michael Beeghly)
Carl H. Lindner
Cincinnati Reds

Clockwise, from top left:

OLYMPIG
Becky Ruehl, 1996 Olympian, Diving
Atkins & Pearce Technology for
Cincinnati 2012, Inc.

WHEN WE WIN THE SUPER BOWL
Kathy Raab
Colliers International

PIG IRON
Michael Keyes
Bonnie and Charlie Moore

SNORT-OINK-EEL
Eric Henn
Newport Aquarium

JAVIER E. JARRIN

At left:

BJORN BOARG
Sarah Thompson
John Tisdel Distributing

Opposite:

TECHNICAL SOW
Toby Lay
Jan and Owen Wrassman for the
Mathis Foundation for Children

56

JAVIER E. JARRIN

It's A Pig Surprise!

A LITTLE BIT OF THIS. A LITTLE BIT OF THAT. SOME OF OUR PIGS WERE HARD

TO CATEGORIZE, BUT EASY TO LOVE.

At left:

JEWELIETTE
Laurie Burnham
Haberer Registered Investments for the
Cincinnati Horticultural Society

59

From left to right:

FRANC PIG YEN DOW
Laurie Burnham
Haberer Registered Investments for
the Cincinnati Horticultural Society

O'PEN...THE PIG IDEA!
The LPK Community
LPK

JAVIER E. JARRIN

JAVIER E. JARRIN

JAVIER E. JARRIN

JAVIER E. JARRIN

Clockwise from top left:

SIX DEGREES OF ...
Mark Fox
Enjoy th Arts/START

A FLY IN THE OINKMENT
Sarah Thompson
Auxiliary of Bethesda Hospitals, Inc.

SHE'S A HONEY
Amy and Matt Corbin
The Honeybaked Ham Company

61

JAVIER E. JARRIN

Clockwise, from top left

RYLEY
Ellen Miller
Ryland Homes

PERIODIC PIG
Amy Kettner
Cognis Corporation

PORK-OPULENCE
Sara Jane Bellamy
Fran and Jim Allen
Cincinnati Ballet

PIGSPECTIVE
Thomas August Renko
Art Opportunities, Inc.

62

PEGGY McHALE

JAVIER E. JARRIN

JAVIER E. JARRIN

JAVIER E. JARRIN

JAVIER E. JARRIN

Top to bottom:

STAINLESS SQUEAL
Jonathan Hand
Ferguson Metals Inc.

ART SPRINGS INTERNAL
Shannon Eakins
Cincinnati Arts Association

THOMAS W. GUENTHER

It's A Pig Surprise!

64

At left:

A PIG FOR ALL SEASONS - SPRING
Michael Scott
Darlene and Jeff Anderson, Melody Richardson and The Otto M. Budig Family Foundation
The Cincinnati Ballet

KELLY BARNHORST-SCHNELLE

Clockwse, from top left:

A PIG FOR ALL SEASONS - AUTUMN
Michael Scott
Darlene and Jeff Anderson, Melody Richardson and The Otto M. Budig Family Foundation for
The Cincinnati Ballet

A PIG FOR ALL SEASONS - WINTER
Michael Scott
Darlene and Jeff Anderson, Melody Richardson and The Otto M. Budig Family Foundation for
The Cincinnati Ballet

A PIG FOR ALL SEASONS - SUMMER
Michael Scott
Darlene and Jeff Anderson, Melody Richardson and The Otto M. Budig Family Foundation for
The Cincinnati Ballet

At left:

CONTEMPORARY ARTS CENTERLOIN
Zaha Hadid
Murray Sinclaire, Jr./Ross, Sinclaire
& Associates, Inc. for the
Contemporary Arts Center

Opposite

MS. PENCILINE
Patrice Trauth and Amy Burton
Ursuline Academy of Cincinnati

66

JAVIER E. JARRIN

JAVIER E. JARRIN

Pigging Out

OUR LITTLE PIGS WENT TO MARKET. SOMETIMES THEY BROUGHT HOME THE BACON, AND SOMETIMES

THEY HAMMED IT UP. A FEW EVEN TOOK AN ALTERNATIVE ROUTE THROUGH THE VEGETABLE PATCH.

JAVIER E. JARRIN

Left to right

COOKING WITH THE PIG AT
bigg's
David Wilson
bigg's Eastgate Hypermarket

Clockwise, from top right:

FOODIE TOOTIE IN THE LAND OF A SOWSAND FOODS
Mary Ann Lederer
Jungle Jim's International Market

CHOICE CUTS
Rebecca Lomax, Patricia Robisch, Sean
Hughes, Geoff Raker
CityBeat

MAISOWNETTE
Lynne, Scott, Steve Hamons
The Maisonette Group

JAVIER E. JARRIN

JAVIER E. JARRIN

JAVIER E. JARRIN

JAVIER E. JARRIN

JAVIER E. JARRIN

Clockwise, from top left:

WAKE UP AND SMELL THE BACON
Lynn Rose
Greater Cincinnati Hotel and Motel Association

THIS LIT'L PIGGY WENT TO REMKE MARKET
Deborah Pille
Remke Markets

HAM & SWISS ON RYE TO GO
Peter N. Kurlas
Plum Street Group

PIG OUT...OFTEN
Liz Kathman Grubow
Greater Cincinnati Restaurant Association

JAVIER E. JARRIN

JAVIER E. JARRIN

At left:

GRILLIN' RIBS
Lynne, Scott, Steve Hamons
JTM Food Group

JAVIER E. JARRIN

JAVIER E. JARRIN

JAVIER E. JARRIN

Clockwise, from top left:

OINK, SUGAR CREEK'S SUGAR FINE SWINE
JoAnn Heurich
Sugar Creek Packing Co.

CINCINNATI CONEY
Emerson Quillin
Gold Star Chili/Blue Grass Quality
Meats/Klosterman Baking Co.

CHAMPIGNE
Jean Robert deCavel
Marilyn and Martin Wade

PORKOPOLIS PATTI, THE PIZZA PURVEYOR
Daniel Shapero
Mio's

JAVIER E. JARRIN

JAVIER E. JARRIN

At right:

SPARKLING SWINE
Matthew Kotlarczyk
Heidelberg Distributing Company

Opposite:

SOW-VATORE PASTAVINO
Mary Beth Dowlin
Karlo's Bistro Italia

JAVIER E. JARRIN

ROBERT A. FLISCHEL

Divine Swine

PIGS PRODDED OUR SPIRITUAL SIDES, DREAMING OF HIGHER CALLINGS AND A PEACEFUL

WORLD. FORGET ABOUT A HOLY COW. WE HAVE A SACRED SOW!

JAVIER E. JARRIN

Previous page:

DARE TO DREAM
Chris Bailey
Communicating Arts Credit Union

Clockwise, from top left:

CUPIG
Millie Kwong & Ann Dury
University of Cincinnati School of Architecture and Interior Design
Concrete Technology, Inc.

ROGER BACON
Students of Maureen Stephan and Fr. Roger Bosse
Roger Bacon High School

CELESTIAL SWINE
Janet Dickert Schlemmer
Executive Benefits, Inc.
The Guardian Life Insurance Co. of America New York, NY

DIVINE SWINE
Fabricia Duell
Christ Church Cathedral

JAVIER E. JARRIN

JAVIER E. JARRIN

JAVIER E. JARRIN

JAVIER E. JARRIN

JAVIER E. JARRIN

JAVIER E. JARRIN

Clockwise, from top left:

IN THE PIGINNING
High School Art Class
McSwain Flooring America for
Cincinnati Hills Christian Academy

THE SACRED SOW
Edward Casagrande of Earth Orchestra
Interior Services Incorporated
The Feng Shui Annex

THE PIG DIPPER
Suzanne Poag
Cincinnati Magazine

PIG OF POSSIBILITIES
Cindy W. MacConnell
Paycor, the Payroll Service Company

JAVIER E. JARRIN

JAVIER E. JARRIN

80

At left:

SPIRIT DANCING PIG
James "Kwame" Clay
Arts Consortium of Cincinnati

Opposite:

PIG BIRD
Leslie Shiels
A Friend of WCET-48
for WCET-48

JAVIER E. JARRIN

Horticultural Hogs

A BUMPER CROP OF BOTANICAL BEAUTIES SPRANG FORTH EVERYWHERE, LIKE DAFFODILS IN SPRING,

CORN IN THE SUMMER, AND PUMPKINS IN THE FALL.

At left:

TOPIGARY
Leslie Shiels
Betsy La Macchia for
The Civic Garden Center

JAVIER E. JARRIN

At left:

THE PARK'S POTTED PIG
Carol Philpott, Sue Brown, Megan Fay
The Kiln at Hyde Park Square

84

JAVIER E. JARRIN

JAVIER E. JARRIN

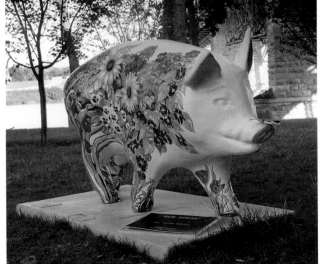

JAVIER E. JARRIN

Clockwise, from top left:

PAINTED PIG
Susan Wechsler
Towne Properties

SOW SPRING
Kathy Sabato
The Longi Family

THE DAYS OF SWINE AND ROSES
Linda Kreidler
Cincinnati International Wine Festival

SOWMMERFAIR
Karen Kelly
Summerfair, Inc.

TONY ARRASMITH

JAVIER E. JARRIN

JAVIER E. JARRIN

JAVIER E. JARRIN

PIGMENT OF OUR IMAGINATION
The "Gems" of Our Community: The Students of Charlotte Skurow and Gail Wissel, assisted by Gayle Shova
Ethicon Endo Surgery, Inc. and

Sycamore Community Schools
Edwin H. Greene Intermediate School, Sycamore Community School District

86

PEACEFUL PIG
Joe Kiefer
Brighton Center

PIG OF THE LITTER
Students of Brenda Tarbell
Jim Tarbell
Annunciation School

TONY ARRASMITH

JAVIER E. JARRIN

JAVIER E. JARRIN

Clockwise, from top left:

DANDELION SWINE
Amanda Hogan
The Shepherd Color Company

PIG-A-LILY
Deirdre Mahne
Smale Family

RESPECT PIG
Mary Ann Lederer
Susan's Natural World/Amy's Natural
Nutrition/Cincinnati Natural
Foods/Clifton Natural
Foods/Toomey Natural Foods

MS. PUERCOZILLA PIGITA PIGGLESWORTH (A.K.A.) SUEE ELEANOR PIGSBY)
Julie A. Burkhardt's Art I, II and III students and Community of NDA
Notre Dame Academy

JAVIER E. JARRIN

JAVIER E. JARRIN

At left:

PLANTAPIGAMONGUS
Ken Page
The Board of Trustees for
The Parks Foundation

Opposite:

UN COCHON DANS LE JARDIN
Paula Ott, Denise Strasser, Sally McLane, Susan Koenig
Tiffany & Co.

JAVIER E. JARRIN

JAVIER E. JARRIN

Pigs with a Purpose

PUTTING OUR PIGS IN THE SPOTLIGHT GAVE SOME OF US THE

OPPORTUNITY TO "SOWND" OFF ON BEHALF OF A CAUSE.

Previous page:

ANGEL
Carole Meyer
Donna L. Stahl, M.D. Inc.
for Breast Cancer Angels, Inc.

Left to right:

THESE LITTLE PIGGIES
Sanger & Eby Design/Patients
Children's Hospital Medical Center

HAMLICH MANEUVRE
Lynn Judd
The Heimlich Institute

92

JAVIER E. JARRIN

JAVIER E. JARRIN

JAVIER E. JARRIN

JAVIER E. JARRIN

Clockwise, from top left:

GOETTA EDUBACON
Students of Janet Gorman
St. Mary School

PIG PALS
Sarah Lahti
KnowledegeWorks Foundation for
Cincinnati Youth Collaborative

PIGANTHROPY
Suzanne L. Fisher
The Greater Cincinnati Foundation

UNTIL THERE'S A CURE
Lauren Hoeffel
AIDS Volunteers of
Cincinnati/Caracole

JAVIER E. JARRIN

JAVIER E. JARRIN

Clockwise, from top left:

HAMS ACROSS AMERICA
Mary Beth Riesenberg, Kathy Raab and Children from BBBS
Albert and Marion Brown, Jr. for Big Brothers Big Sisters of Greater Cincinnati, Inc.

TURPIN SWINE AND SISTER SOWS
Students of Andrea Sloan
Turpin High School

BENCH AND BOAR
Anne Gerhardt
Graydon Head & Ritchey LLP
Cincinnati Bar Foundation

THE ARTS WILL MAKE YOUR PIG FLY
Kerry Kronenberger, Jaye Mullins, Carla Copens and Shawnee Elementary
Association for the Advancement of Arts Education

Opposite:

MR. MEATLESS
Karen Friedman
Animal Rights Community/Cincinnati Vegetarian Resource Group

JAVIER E. JARRIN

JAVIER E. JARRIN

JAVIER E. JARRIN

JAVIER E. JARRIN

JOE HARRISON

Left to right:

A PIGIRL SCOUT'S WORLD
Annie Ruth
Girl Scouts - Great Rivers Council, Inc.

GO VEG PIGGY
Betsy Reeves
People for the Ethical Treatment of Animals

JAVIER E. JARRIN

JAVIER E. JARRIN

JAVIER E. JARRIN

JOE HARRISON

Clockwise, from top left:

A SWINE OF SIGNS
Katherine Ferraro, Sr. Geralyn Schneider, FSM, Sandi Reitz
St. Rita School for the Deaf

GO VEG.COM
Betsy Reeves
People for the Ethical Treatment of Animals

AHIMSA (NON INJURY TO ANY BEING)
Mary Ann Lederer
Earthsave Cincinnati and Farm Sanctuary

JAVIER E. JARRIN

JAVIER E. JARRIN

At left:

NON-PROFIT-PIG
Robert W. Grove
Staley/Robeson/Ryan/St. Lawrence,
Inc.

JAVIER E. JARRIN

JAVIER E. JARRIN

Top to bottom:

**SOW-CIETY FOR THE
PRESERVATION OF
MUSIC HALL**
Joe Foster
Anonymous Donor
for The Society for the Preservation
of Music Hall

CURED HAM SANDWICH
Steve McGowan
Margie Rauh for
Multiple Sclerosis Society

99

100

At left:

FREEDOM PIG -
PIG IN A BLANKET
Jimi Jones
The Citizens' Committee on Youth

ROBERT A. FLISCHEL

Left to right:

PIG BROTHER'S WATCHING
YOU
S.V. Murphree
Media Bridges Cincinnati

ANIMAL HOUSE
Tracey Antoun
xpedx, An International Paper
Company

TONY ARRASMITH

Left to right:

IT'S PIGEMENTARY
Pam Kravetz and Tara Keller
bigg's Hypermarket Harrison for
Whitewater Valley Elementary

THE BABY PORK WITH
ANOTHER SPECIAL DELIVERY
FROM GOOD SAMARITAN
HOSPITAL
Mona Karram
The Good Samaritans

Opposite:

MONTESSO(W)RI AT THE NEW
SCHOOL: PIG IN A (PEACE)
BLANKET
**Robin Hartmann and the Elementary
Students at The New School**
The New School

JAVIER E. JARRIN

JAVIER E. JARRIN

JOE HARRISON

Dressed to the Swines

OUR PIGS PLAYED DRESS-UP AS FAMILIAR CHARACTERS, SOMETIMES IN ROLES

WE ESPECIALLY DREAMED UP FOR THE YEAR 2000. SOME PLAYED OTHER

ANIMALS. AND SOME WERE JUST PIGS.

At left:

PIGTORIA'S SECRET
Heather Chitwood
The Plastic Surgery Group, Food
Specialties, Brendamour and
Lawrence Kurtzman, MD for
The Cincinnati Ballet

105

JAVIER E. JARRIN

JAVIER E. JARRIN

Clockwise, from top left:

SQUEAKY CLEAN
Heather Chitwood
Professional Maintenance of
Cincinnati

JEWELIA PIG
Korin Wulkowicz
Boris Litwin Jewelers

STAGE HAMS
Jay Depenbrock
Cincinnati Stage Employees
Local #5

JAVIER E. JARRIN

JAVIER E. JARRIN

JAVIER E. JARRIN

Clockwise, from top left:

PORK RULES
Claudette Graumlich
John Morrell & Co.

SAKSY BABE
Mark Adams and Bruce Raitch
Saks Fifth Avenue

SHEAKIN' BACON
Amanda and Lynn Hogan
The Sheakley Group of Companies

HOT PIG IN A BLANKET
Louise Niklas
Ruth W. Westheimer and Family

JAVIER E. JARRIN

JAVIER E. JARRIN

Clockwise, from top left:

CIRCLEPORK
Steven Moore
Corporex Companies

MISS SOW JONES 2000
Students of Mason High School
Prudential Securities
Mason High School

THE SILKY SOW WITH
HAM BAG
Floral Designers of the Silky Way
The Silky Way

DUKE OF PORKOPOLIS
Kim Hanrahan
Duke-Weeks Realty Corporation

Opposite:

JUICY LUCY IN THE SKY WITH
DIAMONDS
Dodie Loewe
Richter & Phillips Jewelers

108

KELLY BARNHORST-SCHNELLE

PEGGY McHALE

PEGGY McHALE

TONY ARRASMITH

JAVIER E. JARRIN

At left:

SOW VON CARPENTER
Kathy Sabato
Turner Construction Company

JAVIER E. JARRIN

KELLY BARNHORST-SCHNELLE

KELLY BARNHORST-SCHNELLE

CHRIS CONE

Clockwise, from top left:

MISS PATCHWORK PORK
Ohio River Valley Artists Guild
Maysville-Mason County Tourism
Commission
Ohio River Valley Artists Guild

PORK CHOPPER
Jim "Dauber" Farr
Ferd and Thelma Meinor
Harley-Davidson of Cincinnati, Inc.

PINKY
PHC Group/MKT
Northern Kentucky Convention and
Visitors Bureau

112

JAVIER E. JARRIN

At left:

GLIMMER GLIMMER AND
SWINE
Brian Mehring
Kaplan Foundation for
The Ensemble Theater

JAVIER E. JARRIN

JAVIER E. JARRIN

Clockwise, from top left:

PIGGY IN PIGAMAS
Students of Sylvia Dick and Melba Guard
bigg's for Oakdale Elementary School

JC HAM
Students of Bety Lambert
Hamilton County Juvenile Court for Hillcrest Schools

QUEEN PIGTORIA'S GUARD
Barbara Ahlbrand
Victoria Square

REGINALD, DRESSED TO THE SWINES
Michael Chaney
Haute Chocolate, Inc. And Oswald Company, Inc.

113

JAVIER E. JARRIN

JAVIER E. JARRIN

KELLY BARNHORST-SCHNELLE

Top to bottom:

BLUES BROTHER
Melissa Day
Anthem Blue Cross and Blue Shield

PATSEY - THE PHENOMENAL,
PRANCING, PAISLEY, PIANO-
PLAYING PORKER
Judy Hand
Baldwin Piano Company

114

Opposite:

SUNLITE SOWLY
Cindy Matyi
Coney Island

THOMAS A. GUENTHER

JOE HARRISON

Enlightened Swine

WE SIMPLY GLOWED WHEN WE SAW OUR ILLUMINATED

PIGS. SOMETIMES THEY LIT UP THE NIGHT.

117

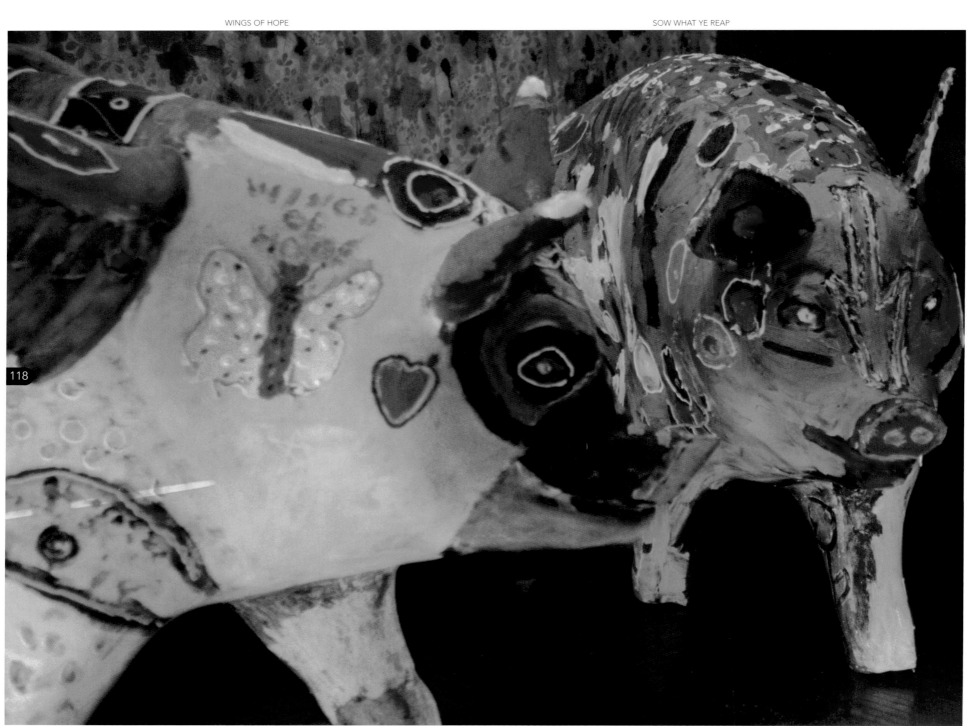

118

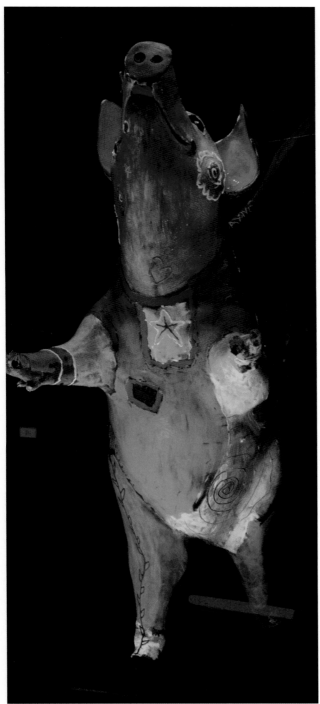

TOM BACHER

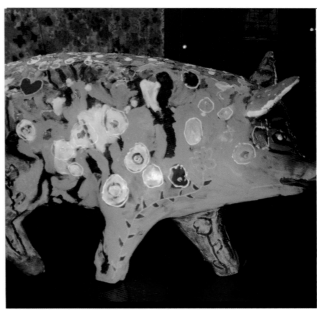

TOM BACHER

Opposite:

WINGS OF HOPE
The Springer School Kids and Tom Bacher
Boys Hope Girls Hope

Left to right:

PIG 4
The Springer School Kids and Tom Bacher
The Lottery Channel

SOW WHAT YE REAP
The Springer School Kids and Tom Bacher
Marilyn and Martin Wade

JAVIER E. JARRIN

JAVIER E. JARRIN

Clockwise, from left to right:

CINSOWNNATI PIG
Mark Eberhard
Firstar Bank

IDEA HOG
Frederic Ellenberger
Northlich

PIGLIT
Cole Carothers
Twink Carothers for
LKC Foundation

COSMIC SWINE
Corbin Lurrie Pomeranz
Steve and Penny Pomeranz &
Family, Cris and Holly Collinsworth
& Family for
Stadium Open M.R.I.

Opposite:

WATT A PIG!
Steve McGowan
Cinergy for
The Wellness Community

JAVIER E. JARRIN

JAVIER E. JARRIN

JAVIER E. JARRIN

Pigs in the City

CINCINNATI, COVINGTON AND NEWPORT LOOK GREAT, IN OUR PIG'S EYES.

OUR SKYLINE AND URBAN VIEWS WERE REFLECTED EVERYWHERE.

123

JAVIER E. JARRIN

Previous page:

SWINESCRAPER
GBBN Architects
GBBN Architects

Left to right:

SOW'S IT GOIN,' CINCINNATI?
Bev Kirk
J.C. Bradford & Co. for the
Mathis Foundation for Children

PIG WORKS
Katie Foertsch
Waite, Schneider, Bayless, &
Chesley

JAVIER E. JARRIN

JAVIER E. JARRIN

JAVIER E. JARRIN

JAVIER E. JARRIN

JAVIER E. JARRIN

JAVIER E. JARRIN

Clockwise, from top left:

BOAR-TENDER
Emerson Quillin
Greater Cincinnati Hotel and Motel
Association

ALL-A-BOAR-D!
John A. Ruthven
Cincinnati Museum Center

ORANGE BARROW, THE
ROAD HOG
Lynn Judd
Stanley and Frances Cohen

PIG IN THE PARK - PARK ON
THE PIG
Students of Wylie Ferguson
Louise Taft Semple Foundation for
Aiken High School/Walnut Hills
High School

125

Clockwise, from top left:

SUNDAY DRIVE PIG
Douglas P. Smith
Klosterman Baking Company

MASON DIXON SWINE
Suzanne L. Fisher
ArtWorks

PRESERVATION PIG
Chuck Marshall
Cincinnati Preservation Association

SCRIPPSOWARD
Emerson Quillin
Scripps Howard Foundation

JAVIER E. JARRIN

JAVIER E. JARRIN

JAVIER E. JARRIN

JAVIER E. JARRIN

At left:

STYLER DAVIDSON SOW-TAIN
Lynne, Scott, Steve Hamons
Jack Rouse Associates

JAVIER E. JARRIN

Left to right:

PORKOPOLIS
Steed Hammond Paul
Steed Hammond Paul

HOGTOBERFEST
Team 8-5, 1999-2000
Nagel Middle School, Forest Hills
School District

JAVIER E. JARRIN

JAVIER E. JARRIN

JAVIER E. JARRIN

JAVIER E. JARRIN

Clockwise, from top left:

QUEEN PORKTUNIA
Bill Seitz
Greater Cincinnati Convention and
Visitors Bureau

HOOSIER HAMPSHIRE
Students of Ruth Ann Batta
bigg's Hypermarket for
Sunman Elementary

PORK OF ENTRY
S.V. Murphree
SENCORP

PIG IN THE CITY
Kendle Corporate Communications
Kendle International Inc.

JAVIER E. JARRIN

JAVIER E. JARRIN

130

KELLY BARNHORST-SCHNELLE

At left:

THE CITY OF NEWPORK
The Artery (Laura Hollis)
City of Newport

JAVIER E. JARRIN

JAVIER E. JARRIN

Clockwise, from top left:

OINKITECTURE
Eric Franke
Michael Schuster Associates

QUEEN PIGGY OF THE WEST
Hans Papke
Cincinnati Financial Corporation/The
Cincinnati Insurance Companies

PADDLE SQUEALER
Chris Reiff
William M. Mercer, Incorporated

PEGGY McHALE

132

At left:

EDEN PORK
Jan Brown Checco
BMF Board of Trustees
BMF Pediatric Care

JAVIER E. JARRIN

KELLY BARNHORST-SCHNELLE

Clockwise, from top left:

A WALK IN THE PORK
Sally Wellington Dodge
Closson's

PIG IN A BLANKET
Deborah L. Ward
Stephen and Inez Allen
CTS Packaging, Inc.

WELCOME TO NEWPORK -
THE VIEW'S GREAT
Ryan Schwass
SENCORP

KELLY BARNHORST-SCHNELLE

134

Previous spread:

DUAL PORCINEALITY (NAMED
BY LEE ANN BUSKIRK)
Jim Borgman
The Cincinnati Enquirer

Left to right:

THE GREAT CINCINNATI PIG
*Kilgour Students Grades K-6 of
Darlene Nored*
Kilgour PTA
Kilgour Elementary School

A PIG'S TALE: HISTORY ON
THE HOOF
Lisa Gillham
Adams Stepner, Waltermann &
Dusing/CBC Foundation,
Inc./Fabulous Furs/The
Madison/Loft Development/Mind &
Matter Gallery/Motch Jewelers/Old
Town Cafe/The Point Restaurant &
Catering/McDaniels Interiors/Kirby-
Mizak Advertising/Bogart
Productions

Opposite:

PIGLENIUM
David Laug
Bruce A. Cook, Inc.

TOM GUENTHER

KELLY BARNHORST-SCHNELLE

KELLY BARNHORST-SCHNELLE

Hams

MAYBE MISS PIGGY STARTED IT ALL. REGARDLESS, OUR PIGS WERE ALL

A LITTLE STAR-STRUCK.

JAVIER E. JARRIN

Previous page:

FRANKENSWINE
Robert Schafer
The Pomeranz Family
Proscan Imaging

Left to right:

SENATOR PIG
Students of Constance Gilbert
Louise Taft Semple Foundation
for Taft High School

PORKEMON
Wayne Clark
Lazarus

JAVIER E. JARRIN

JAVIER E. JARRIN

JAVIER E. JARRIN

JAVIER E. JARRIN

Clockwise, from top left:

ARMORED HAMMER
Thomas Hieronymus Towhey
Federation Antiques Inc.

LEADER-HOGEN CINCINNATI
Carrie Lynn Cooke
Leadership Cincinnati Alumni
Association

PORKUS WELBY, M.D.
Christine M. Bieri
UC Physicians

141

JAVIER E. JARRIN

Left to right:

THE PHANTOM OF THE
SLOPERA
Lisa Molyneux
Fifth Third Bank Broadway Series

DONALD RUMP,
PYGMALION-AIRE
Barbara W. Trauth
Keating Lame Roe

Opposite:

TUTANKHAMUN
Halena Cline
Schiff, Kreidler-Shell Insurance

142

JAVIER E. JARRIN

JAVIER E. JARRIN

143

Left to right:

PIG BOY
Clifton Lin
Frisch's Big Boy Restaurants

SHAZHAM
Patricia A. Renick
Harkavy Family

JAVIER E. JARRIN

JAVIER E. JARRIN

JAVIER E. JARRIN

JAVIER E. JARRIN

145

JAVIER E. JARRIN

146

At left:

CARMINE SWINE
David Flege
Carl H. Lindner
Chiquita Brands International

KELLY BARNHORST-SCHNELLE

JAVIER E. JARRIN

Clockwise, from top left:

UNCLE HAM
Heather Chitwood
Peoples Bank of Northern Kentucky

PORKHOS
Brian Haberski and Richard Schilling
Xavier University

AUSTIN SOWERS
Brian Paden
The Zaring Family Foundation

SHOGUN
Cole Carothers
Klinedinst Family

JAVIER E. JARRIN

KELLY BARNHORST-SCHNELLE

Left to right:

MAD SWINE-TIST
Daniel R. Shapero
BIO/START

THE SOWTUE OF LIBERTY
Susan Siegman and Karen Ballinger
AAA Cincinnati

Opposite:

PIG-MALION
Lisa Molyneux
Cincinnati Playhouse in the PORK

148

KELLY BARNHORST-SCHNELLE

ROBERT A. FLISHEL

JAVIER E. JARRIN

In the Playpen

SOMETIMES CINCINNATIANS ARE A LITTLE TOO SERIOUS. OUR PIGS SHOWED

US THE VALUE OF A GOOD SENSE OF HUMOR.

151

Previous page:

HOG WILD
Cindy Hackney
Williams Family

Clockwise, from top left:

PORKY PLAY'A
Students of Bill Thomas
Louise Taft Semple Foundation
for Woodward High School

PIGGY-GO-ROUND
Joseph Edwin Smith
Rotary Club of Cincinnati
Rotary Foundation of Cincinnati

PIG OUT ON PLASTICS
Mark Eberhard
Milacron, Inc.

SQUEAL OF FORTUNE
Deborah L. Ward
Susie Gaynor/Maureen Pippin

Opposite:

BABES IN TOYLAND
Bang Zoom Design Ltd.
Bang Zoom Design Ltd.

152

JAVIER E. JARRIN

ROBERT A. FLISCHEL

JAVIER E. JARRIN

JAVIER E. JARRIN

153

154

JAVIER E. JARRIN

At left:

PULLED PORK
Richard Groot and the Deskey Staff
Deskey, Integrated Branding

JAVIER E. JARRIN

JAVIER E. JARRIN

Clockwise, from top left:

PIG-TAC-TOE
Jonathan Hand
The Folgers Coffee Company

SOW POWER
Ursula Roma
YWCA

I SQUEAL, YOU SQUEAL, WE ALL SQUEAL FOR ICE CREAM
Ms. Heather K. Bollen and Indian Hill Middle School Art Students
United Dairy Farmers for Indian Hill Middle School-Art Department

MARBELIZED PIG-MENT
Tanya Pfeffer-Witzell
Rosemary and Frank Bloom

JAVIER E. JARRIN

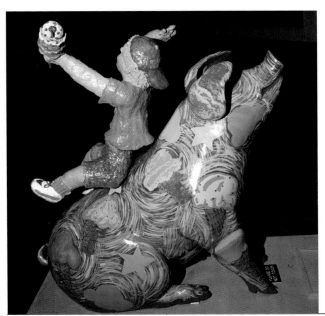

JAVIER E. JARRIN

Clockwise, from top left:

UPERSE IGPE, THE PIG LATIN
PIG
Students of Terri Schatzman
Dixie Heights High School
Clockwise, from top left:

HAM 'N' EGGS
Students of Jody Knoop
John Brooks
7 Hills (Lotspiech)

PIGBIRD
Jeff Hensley and Kevin O'Grady
KFORCE.COM
Archbishop Moeller High School

KELLY BARNHORST-SCHNELLE

JAVIER E. JARRIN

JAVIER E. JARRIN

JAVIER E. JARRIN

Clockwise, from top left:

HOG WASH
Jill Dehener
Steve Fischer

CONSTRUCTION PORKER
Connie Toelke
Frank Messer & Sons Construction Co.

KING MILLIE
Students of Katie Mason
Kings Mills Elementary PTO
Kings Mills Elementary

ALPHAPIGABET
Mrs. Betsy Terrill and her 4th Grade Art Students
bigg's
Symmes Elementary,
Sycamore Schools

157

JAVIER E. JARRIN

JAVIER E. JARRIN

Clockwise, from top left:

PIG LATIN
Frank Herrmann
Frost & Jacobs LLP

HAMLITE
Margaret Wenstrup
D. L. Schiff

HAND OVER 'DA PIG!
Students of Amy Renner Lampe
Paine Webber, Skyline Chili, Attach
Mate, Delhi Nursery, Springdale
Elementary P.T.A.
Springdale Elementary School

JAVIER E. JARRIN

JAVIER E. JARRIN

JAVIER E. JARRIN

TONY ARRASMITH

PEGGY McHALE

PORKER'S WILD
The U.S. Playing Card Company Art Department
The U.S. Playing Card Company

PIGNATA
Marilyn Wade
Marilyn and Martin Wade

HOG TIED
Art Students of Vicki Lanzador, Grades 1-3
Ayer Student Council
Ayer Elementary

THE PIGGEST SHOW ON EARTH
Ruth Levinson
Ruth Levinson for
Juvenile Diabetes Foundation

159

TONY ARRASMITH

JAVIER E. JARRIN

PIGTURE PORKFECT
Art Students of Vicki Lanzador, Grades 4-6
Ayer PTA
Ayer Elementary

Left to right:

POINKY PIG
Barry Gunderson
Irwin Weinberg
Assistance in Marketing Inc.

Opposite:

ONE SWINE DAY IN MAY
Hans Papke
14 Mainstrasse Village Businesses

JAVIER E. JARRIN

KELLY BARNHORST-SCHNELLE

JAVIER E. JARRIN

The Legend of
Sleepy Wallow
and other great works of literature

WHAT'S THE GOOD WORD? NO MATTER HOW WE SPELLED IT,

THIS YEAR IT PROBABLY RHYMED WITH "PIG".

At left:

WONDERFUL WILBUR
Michelle Schuler
Bob and Sandy Heimann

163

Clockwise, from top left:

PIGTALES
Carla Copens/Pam Kravetz/Karen Saunders
Nancy and David Wolf

I SPY PIG
Kathy Robertson McCord
Sally and Holden Wilson, Jr./
Jan and Owen J. Wrassman for
BMF Pediatric Care

THERE'S NO PLACE LIKE HAM
Lynn Hogan
John T. Reis

JAVIER E. JARRIN

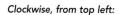

Clockwise, from top left:

THE THREE LITTLE PIGS:
HOUSE OF BRICKS
Jan. Marx Knoop
The Donovan Family

THE THREE LITTLE PIGS:
HOUSE OF STRAW
Jan. Marx Knoop
Chris and Jim Geier

THE THREE LITTLE PIGS:
HOUSE OF STICKS
Jan. Marx Knoop
Jo Joseph

JAVIER E. JARRIN

JAVIER E. JARRIN

166

PLEASE DO
NOT TOUCH

At left:

CHESHIRE PIG
Steve and Rokeya Brauch
Convergys

JAVIER E. JARRIN

JAVIER E. JARRIN

Clockwsie, from top left:

SOWMWHERE OVER THE RAINBOW
Students of Susan Vater
Chumbley-Rankle Construction for Anderson High School

HAMLET
Brian Heim
A Friend of CSF for Cincinnati Shakespeare Festival

HAMINGWAY
Employees of Joseph-Beth
Joseph-Beth Booksellers

THE LIBOARY PIG: PIG OUT ON BOOKS
David Rohs
Public Library of Cincinnati and Hamilton County

JAVIER E. JARRIN

JAVIER E. JARRIN

At left:

PIG IN THE SKY
Sharon Pennekamp
College of Mount St. Joseph

Opposite:

HOGWARTS FROM THE HARRY POTTER BOOKS
Liz DuQuette and 8th Grade Honors Students
Rumpke Waste Removal Systems
Pleasant Run Middle School

JAVIER E. JARRIN

JAVIER E. JARRIN

Pigs in Space

FLYING PIGS WERE OUR TAKE-OFF POINT. SO NATURALLY OUR PIGS WERE

IN MOTION, SOMETIMES VERTICALLY, SOMETIMES HORIZONTALLY.

At left:

PIGASUS
Lynn Judd
Creekwood Construction

171

Left to right:

LEONARDO'S WHIRLY PIG
Stephen Geddes
Delta Air Lines
Neediest Kids of All

THE PIG BANG THEORY
Gary Gaffney
Planet Products

172

JAVIER E. JARRIN

JAVIER E. JARRIN

JAVIER E. JARRIN

JAVIER E. JARRIN

Left to right:

LEONARDO'S FLYING PIG
Sheri Besso
Art Academy of Cincinnati

AMELIA PIGART
Students of Jennifer Drydyk
Amelia High School

173

At left:

THE PIGAMORE AVIATOR
Students of Mrs. Katy Hall
The Montgomery Elementary PTO
Montgomery Elementary

JAVIER E. JARRIN

JAVIER E. JARRIN

At left:

MUDGELLAN
David Tunison
Discovery Channel

THE SPIRIT OF PIGCINNATI
Patricia A. Renick
Lois and Richard Rosenthal
Foundation

175

At right:

PIG IN SPACE
Elissa Mays - Mercer Students
bigg's - Sky Top Plaza for
Mercer Elementary

Opposite:

TAKING FLIGHT ON THE
SILVER KNIGHT
*Students of Gloria Brinkman,
Jan Harbolt, Mark Wiesner and
Paula Yarnell*
The Summit Country Day School

JAVIER E. JARRIN

Musical Pigs

OUR PIGS MADE BEAUTIFUL MUSIC ALL OVER TOWN,

SINGING, PLAYING AND DANCING FROM OUR

IMAGINATION INTO OUR HEARTS.

Previous page:

SWINE LAKE (HOOFANOVA)
(#1)
T.A. Boyle
The Otto M. Budig Family
Foundation for
The Cincinnati Ballet

SWINE LAKE (SWINE-HILDA)
(#2)
T.A. Boyle
Richardson McKinney, Reba St. Clair,
James & Vivian Schwab, and
Hi-Tech Printing Services, Inc. for
The Cincinnati Ballet

SWINE LAKE (ODETTE)(#3)
T.A. Boyle
Gordon and Nadine Brunner for
The Cincinnati Ballet

SWINE LAKE (PORKISKAYA)
(#4)
T.A. Boyle
Melody Sawyer Richardson for
The Cincinnati Ballet

SWINE LAKE (ODILE) (#5)
T.A. Boyle
Harry and Linda Fath for
The Cincinnati Ballet

JAVIER E. JARRIN

JAVIER E. JARRIN

JAVIER E. JARRIN

JAVIER E. JARRIN

Opposite, clockwise, from top left:

OINKAPPELLA
Steve Johnston, Nancy Pace, Mary Ann Schlotman, Christy Sheppard, Julie Stephens
Union Central Insurance and Investments

PAGANINI PIG, A.K.A. PIGANINI
Greg Penner
Jim Lopata for
The Happy Pig Collectors Club

HAMMIN' ON MAIN
Barbara Ahlbrand
Pepsi-Cola General Bottlers, Inc.
(Jim Flood)

MR. CHOPS
Don Hoffmann
Firstar Bank for
Friends of the Pops

At left:

PIGLIACCI
Christine M. Bieri
Jack and Moe Rouse for
WGUC-FM Radio

JAVIER E. JARRIN

Left to right:

MAESTRO PORKO
Eric Reed Greiner
Mayfield Clinic and Spine Institute
for the May Festival

HIP HOP HOG
Adam Mysock
Walnut Hills High School Alumni
Foundation
Walnut Hills High School

JAVIER E. JARRIN

JAVIER E. JARRIN

JAVIER E. JARRIN

JAVIER E. JARRIN

183

JAVIER E. JARRIN

Left to right:

COUNTRY HAM PIG
Lynn Rose
Tom, Francie, Allison, Andy & Peter
Hiltz

PIGLIACCI
Lynn Judd and Margaret Lewis
Ted Silberstein and Jackie Mack

JAVIER E. JARRIN

JAVIER E. JARRIN

THOMAS W. GUENTHER

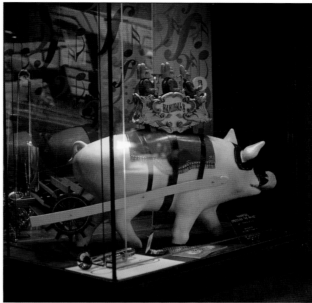

JAVIER E. JARRIN

Clockwise, from top left:

SWINEPHONY
Josh Thompson (designer) and Judy Davis (sculptor)
Symphony Communications

HAMMIBAL CROSSING THE RHINE
Stephen Geddes
The Corbett Foundation
American Classical Music Hall of Fame

ELVIS PIGSLEY
Michael Beeghly, Carissa Barnard, Michael Chaney
FRCH Design Worldwide/Kohnen & Patton LLP/Rippe & Kingston Co. PSC

185

JAVIER E. JARRIN

186

JAVIER E. JARRIN

At left:

HAMSTRINGS
Grace Chin
Frank Messer & Sons Construction
Company
Cincinnati Symphony Orchestra

PEGGY McHALE

JAVIER E. JARRIN

Clockwsie, from top left:

GOING FOR BOAROQUE
Judi Cettel and Beth Eline and Art Students
Prudential Securities for the Cincinnati Chamber Orchestra

LITTLE DRUMMER BOAR
Jennifer Zimmerman
New England Financial

PIG 'O MY HEART
Maureen Gregory and Beth Wexler
St. Columban School

JAVIER E. JARRIN

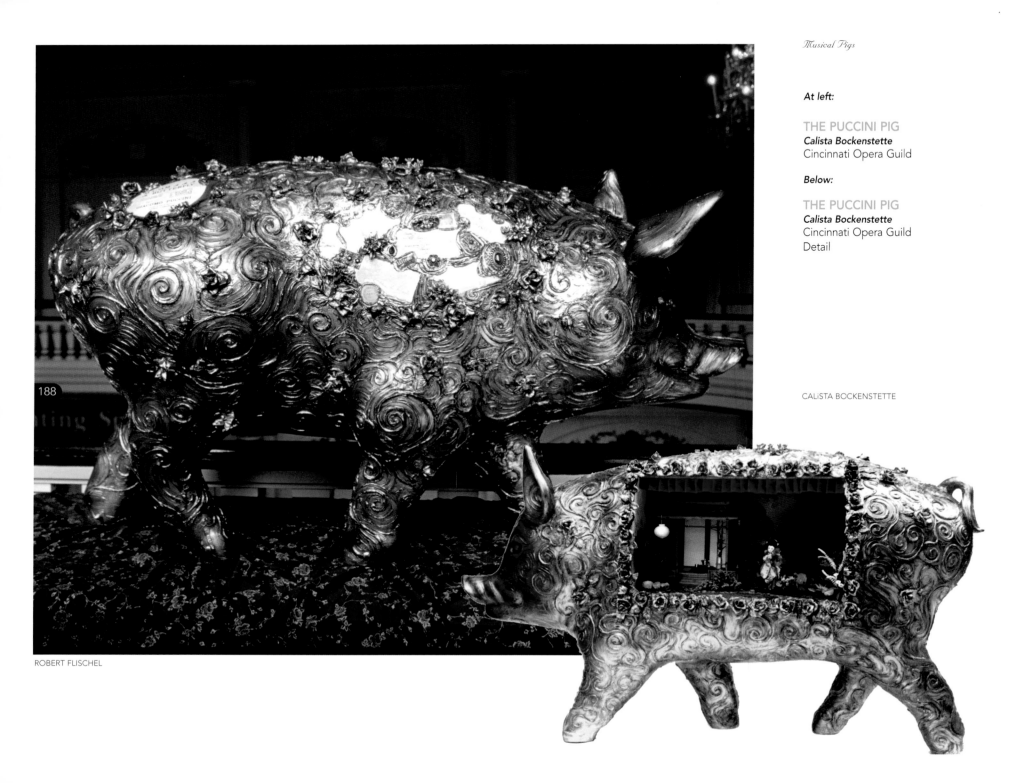

At left:

THE PUCCINI PIG
Calista Bockenstette
Cincinnati Opera Guild

Below:

THE PUCCINI PIG
Calista Bockenstette
Cincinnati Opera Guild
Detail

CALiSTA BOCKENSTETTE

188

ROBERT FLISCHEL

TOM GUENTHER

Left:

DON PIGIOVANNI
Scott Jones
David C. Herriman for
Department for Community Based
Services

Left to right:

PARROTHEAD PIG
David Flege
Riverbend

HI! I'M ARTIE DE OINK, SEE
ME AT ART LINKS!
Linda Mitchell
Art Links

JAVIER E. JARRIN

JAVIER E. JARRIN

JAVIER E. JARRIN

At left:

CHORUSOW (#1)
Cooki Thier
Betsy Young
May Festival

TENORLOIN (#2)
Cooki Thier
Margie and Larry Kyte
May Festival

ALTOINK (#3)
Cooki Thier
Warners
May Festival

SOWPRANO (#4)
Cooki Thier
Cynthia and Rick Muhlhauser
May Festival

BOARITONE (#5)
Cooki Thier
Len and Sherie Marek
May Festival

At right:

BIG NUTCRACKER BOY

Chris Payne
Blanche F. Maier
The Cincinnati Ballet

Opposite:

JIGGIN' PIGGY

Cindy Matyi
Cincinnati Folk Life/The Dubliner
Irish Pub

JAVIER E. JARRIN

JAVIER E. JARRIN

I moved to Cincinnati 20 years ago, and Cincinnati seemed like a pretty uptight place, without much of a sense of humor. In the early 1980s I was scoffed at for suggesting an organization I belonged to should change its annual awards program to the "Porkopolis Awards," an idea I thought was rather clever. Cincinnatians were not amused by their porcine past, I learned, and didn't especially want to be reminded of it. Besides, I was told, those pigs were filthy animals.

An Afterword on Pigs

In 1988, for Cincinnati's Bicentennial we memorialized our feelings about pigs with a big fracas over the flying pigs on Andrew Leicester's statuary for the entrance to Sawyer Point. I rolled my eyes at the time over the fact that we're so inclined to get our shorts in a bunch over the silliest things. But I guessed the advice I'd been given about steering clear of pigs was sound.

So when people started advancing the idea of decorated pigs as a public art project — even given the success of cows in Chicago — I was dubious. But many people were moving in the same positive directions, and it seemed like something everyone might rally around. A lot of people close to me were involved in planning the project, and it really began to take on momentum. My doubts began to dwindle.

As someone who's worked with the arts for a long time, I was excited that the project would showcase many of the fine artists in Greater Cincinnati and Northern Kentucky. I stepped up to get even more involved: An organization I belong to decided to sponsor a pig. I became the liaison with the artist we selected, a creative young woman who teaches high school art. She and her husband worked very hard to create the pig design we chose.

When the pig was finished, I was invited to the artist's home, miles north of downtown Cincinnati, for a sort of open house/farewell to the pig/picnic. He was bolted to their dining room floor, the first thing you saw when you walked in through their front door. As the representative of the sponsor, I was treated royally, greeted and introduced to the artist's parents, grandparents, in-laws, friends, and neighbors. Even to several members of her husband's softball team. They'd all come to share some ownership in this pig because they'd watched it become real.

It was then that the impact of the pigs as a community strength-

PHOTO: JANET HILL-SMITH

ening activity really began to dawn on me. I thought of the roughly 400 pigs and their many artists. It occurred to me that such parties must be happening all over Cincinnati and Northern Kentucky in the spring of 2000, as artists prepared to turn their charges over to ArtWorks for display over the summer. The pigs brought people together and showed us how much fun the arts can be.

Still, when I attended Kahn's "World's Largest Pignic" in June, I wasn't yet appreciating how much good will and community spirit our pigs could generate. On Fountain Square that day I saw the best cross-section of our community I've ever witnessed at an event of any kind. Young adults with kids. Senior citizens. Slackers with tattoos and pierced whatevers. Families. Blacks and whites. People in wheelchairs. Everybody was wandering around, snapping photos, smiling and saying, "Isn't this great?" and "Aren't we proud our city's done such a good job with these pigs?"

OK, I thought. We're impressed with ourselves. But I was really convinced on a sunny Saturday in July. I was hanging out in the Fifth Street atrium at the Westin Hotel when three generations of a family walked by. Granddad was videotaping his son-in-law pushing his granddaughter in a stroller in front of several pigs. I struck up a conversation with the older man and learned he was here from California. His daughter's family lives in Dayton, so he's been to Ohio before, but not to Cincinnati. He saw a story on CBS Sunday Morning about the Big Pig Gig, and decided to make the trip to Dayton so he could bring the whole family to Cincinnati and look around. "Nice city you have here" he told me.

I'd been waiting at the Westin to give a tour to members of the Happy Pig Collectors, a bunch of fanatical folks who fill their homes and lives with all things pig-like. They chose Cincinnati for their annual meeting this year because of the Gig, and they wanted to be shown around. We walked down Fourth Street to Lytle Park, then back to Fountain Square.

They went on and on about our city, and especially about the creativity of our artists. They asked me why more people don't come to visit Cincinnati, although on that pleasant Saturday it was hard to envision having too many more visitors. Downtown was crawling with people studying maps of where the pigs could be found and walking up one street and down another.

When they got tired, they gravitated back to Fountain Square, where they could cool off in the mists of the Tyler Davidson Fountain, all spiffed up after her 18-month rehabilitation.

That's when it hit me, seeing what our city has to offer through the eyes of people from somewhere else. Cincinnati is a great town. What's more, we have great people who live here and work hard to keep making it an even greater place. Not necessarily the business guys or the politicians or any of our so-called leaders. The Big Pig Gig succeeded because lots of people — artists, volunteers, teachers, kids... everyday people — pitched in and did their best. Call it a herd mentality, if you will, but it made me feel downright warm and fuzzy (or was it pink and cuddly?) about our hometown.

Kind of funny, I thought. A bunch of pigs convinced me that Cincinnati, my adopted hometown, is one great place. Know what? I don't think I'm the only one who came to that conclusion.

— Rick Pender

Index by artist

Index by sponsor

Pigs under construction

We regret that the following pigs were not completed in time to make the publication date for this book.

KnowledgeWorks Foundation for
School for Creative and Performng Arts
Bryan Johnson and Ezra Bolotin
HERMES: MESSENGER FOR THE GODS

Robbins Sports Surfaces
Eric Reed Greiner
SLAM-JAM SUEY

Jim Lopata for
The Happy Pig Collectors Club
Greg Penner
ANNE-SOWPHIE MUTTER

marchFIRST
Kathy Raab
DIGITAL SWINE

Monnie & O'Conner Co. L.P.A.
Vanessa Holt
INDUSTRIAL REVOLUTIONARY PIG

Jake Sweeney Automotive
Sarah D. Sweeney
JAKE SWINEY'S BOARVETTE

Ohio Humanities Council
Stephanie Gau
HAMANITIES

Barry I. Randman Family
Frederic Bonin-Pissarro
PIGSSARRO

Zumbiel Packaging
Nolan Ellis
THE OTHER WHITE MEAT

Schering-Plough/Roche for The Barrett Cancer
Cindi Sanders
WORLD PEACE PIG

Harkavy Family
Ben Sloan, Matt Kotlarczyk and Tamara Harkavy
ONE THOUSAND ONE ARABIHAM NIGHTS

GE Aircraft Engines
Chris Bailey
POWERFUL PIG

Cincinnatus Association
Eric Reed Greiner
LUCIUS (LUCKY) QUINCTUS PIGASUS

Ohio Bicentennial Commission
Grace Chin
PIGCENTENNIAL BARN

Joanie and Lou Lauch for Kentucky Building Maintenance, Inc.
Kathy Sabato and Deb Thompson
HAMELA LEE, STAR OF HOGWATCH

Emmalee Greiner
Eric Reed Greiner
PIGPLANT

LaRosa's Pizzerias
Kurt Nicaise
PIZZA PIGNIC

Castellini Foundation
Joe Carr
ESCAPE FROM FINDLAY MARKET

Friends of Findlay, City of Cincinnati/Market Facilities
Suzanna Terrill
HAMBRIEL (GUARDIAN OF GOD'S GARDENS)

Ayer Elementary
Art Students of Vicki Lanzador
AYER ELEMENTARY'S SELF-PORKTRAIT

The Drees Company
Mark Kerley and Sean Petzinger
HOMER

The Montgomery Inn for Sycamore Junior High
8th Grade Artists
THE RIB KING

The Lawfirm of Wood & Lamping LLP
Josiane Trageser
PIG APPEAL

Al Neyer, Inc.
Rob Thrun & Team
SQUEAL ESTATE DEVELOPER

Cincinnati Bell
Chris Daniel
HOG WIRE

Estelle G. Walgreen
Ricki Wagner
FLOWER-POWER PIG

Chancellor Media Corp.- WUBE
Dixie Chicks
WUBE PIG

Mr. and Mrs. Thomas Crain for Cincinnati Opera
Liz Kathman Grubow
PIGALETTO

The Huntington National Bank
Vanessa Holt
FINE SWINE

NATIONAL MARKETSHARE GROUP inc.
Kelly Romer and Susanna Rosenthal
PEDDLER PIG

Patrick Lindsay and Dan McKenna
Cathy Wash and Ryan Lindsay
WHEN IRISH STY'S ARE SMILING

Drackett Design and Antiques
Elaine Finn
HAMTIQUES

Merrill Lynch & Co. for Beech Acres
Marlene Steele
PIGGISH ON AMERICA

National Art Honor Society/Citize
Highlands High SchStudents of Erin NHighland
LASSIE PIG

Junior League of Cincinnati
Sheryl Felner
I'LL COOK WHEN PIGS FLY

Ruth Sawyer
TBD
TBD

Target for Ayer Elementary
Art Students of Vicki Lanzador
BOAR'S EYE (RIGHT ON TARGET)

Johnston Family for Withrow High School and Artworks
Melissa Assum
TBD

Historic Licking Riverside Civic Association
Vernon Rader
SWINE AND ROSES

Warsteiner
Hans Papke
ANDY WARHOL-STEINER PIGGY

Sur-Seal
Ximena and Paulina Flores
ECCO: PIG ON EARTH

Robert I. Stern Family Trust
Janice Ash
TBD

Pierre Foods
Abby Byland
CHEF PIGERRE

Clubhead Records
TBD
TBD

The Carl H. Lindner Family American Jumping Classic
for Shriners Burns Hospital
Lynn Judd
EQUINE SWINE

R.L. Polk & Company
Jeff Hannigan
CHECKERS THE CINCINNATI PIG

University of Cincinnati College of Design, Art, Architecture
and Planning Alumni Governing Board
Shawna Haas and Todd Lang
PIG - SWINE DESIGN

Owen Wrassman
TBD
TBD

Janell, Inc.
James A. Markle
PIG-CRETELY YOURS

Arlene and Bill Katz
Barbara Patterson
IN A PIG'S EYE

Enerfab Inc.
Stephen Geddes
SWINE STEIN

Marilyn and Martin Wade
Mark Wellage

A PIGTURE IS WORTH A THOUSAND WORDS
Covington Community Center, Inc./Mainstrasse Village
Association/Mainstrasse Neighbors Association
Molly and Nathan Bach/Breda Zechmeister

RISIN' SWINE
WSTR-TV (WB64)
Angela Young
WB64 FROG HOG

Berman Printing Co.
Kenn Tompos and Lisa Ballard
INKY STINKY

Over-the-Rhine Foundation
Suzanna Terrill
UBER DER RHEIN SCHWEIN

Saint Ursula Academy
Students of Mary Sue Markey
WINGED PIGTORY

oink!